Hail
Marys

Pat Edwards

Infinity Books UK

First published in Great Britain by Infinity Books UK

Copyright © Infinity Books UK

The moral right of the author has been asserted.

ISBN 9798367217568

www.infinitybooksuk.com

For all the Marys, especially the many, many more I could have written about - maybe next time.

Contents

Naming

Before the spark you were nothing,
and nothing dare exist.
You were not even a thought,
an empty space; nothing is nothing.

Then you became something by chance,
a combination of fire and stars;
a beginning growing,
turning into itself.

And now we must name you,
more than *infant* or *child*;
give you label and title
so you are distinct, recognisable.

We choose *Mary*, in remembrance;
Mary trips off the tongue in blue robes,
head bowed, halo-glimmered,
hands held in prayer.

Or *Mary*, on your father's side,
who made and lost a fortune,
or who was a nurse in the war,
or who saw ghosts and demons.

Or another *Mary*, beloved,
forgotten until now,
resurrected in your cries,
your curls, your damp skin.

Before the spark you were nothing,
a sleeping name waiting to be fire and stars,
growing into something,
turning into *Mary*.

Virgin

She wears sandals and loose clothing, dusty from walking to fetch water.
The young men stare, peel away another layer of her childhood.

She senses she is not alone, thinks that one of them has followed her,
glances over her shoulder, just the shadow of his motion in the trees.

She stops at the crossroads, pulls up her robes to rest on haunches,
wipes a little sweat from her brow with the back of her brown hand.

She feels he is closer now, behind that stone or by the broken gate,
but she dare not look up, gathers herself to walk on, chest fluttering.

She draws the water, feels it's weight inhabit stone flasks like worries
when they fill a girl's heart. Today she is careless and distracted.

She shocks herself back to her task, kicks earth over the spillage,
begins the journey home. Now she sees him and their eyes lock.

She walks more quickly, is home, stows away the flasks in the cool,
goes to lie down on the bed. She strokes the mound of her abdomen.

She finds the journeys longer, the flasks heavier, the work a chore.
Each day she fills and fills, feels their stares ageing her like water marks.

She throws up by the broken gate, uses her sleeve to clean her mouth.
The young men talk about her, seeing her so changed and flushed.

She tells her mother she can't fetch water today, she is too unwell.
She carries a weight heavier than any flask, fuller than a worried heart.

She is breached, empties her flask in a mighty gush like a holy deluge, kicks
sand over the spillage and tells everyone she doesn't understand.

Mary the Blessed Virgin
The Bible tells us that Jesus, Son of God, was born to a virgin by immaculate
conception; that Mary was visited by the Holy Spirit and became pregnant without
intercourse. This poem imagines a young girl living in a rural, under-developed
region. What if such a girl fell pregnant, at the hands of a man from her village, as she
walked to fetch water? What if she became the focus of some story about a divine
birth, and rumours spread that her son was destined to save the world?

The two Marys meet for a catch up

They agreed to meet in a well-known coffee shop,
Mary M in sunglasses, the older Mary avoiding blue.
They ordered flat whites, agreed to share a Hot Cross Bun.

The older Mary said they'd named a prayer after her;
Mary M said she's heard about a song in a musical,
something about not knowing how to love him.

There were many silences between them,
moments pregnant with just what to say.
Mary M tried to lighten the atmosphere.

Have you seen him, she said, jerking her head
towards the Barista. He was about thirty something,
with one of those fashionable beards. Nothing.

Mary M made her excuses and headed for the loo.
On the way, the Barista asked, do you fancy
meeting up later for supper or a drink.

Mary M said not really, I'm washing my hair;
besides Sundays are never really very good for me.
When she returned, older Mary had vanished.

Mary M enjoyed the smell of spices in her bun,
the oily feel of butter melting on her fingers.
As she bit in, she left the red of her mouth on the bread.

Mary Magdalene was a woman said to have followed Jesus,
even to have witnessed his death and miraculous reappearance
in the garden a few days later. She is often portrayed as a
prostitute who washed Jesus's feet with oil and spices.

Losing her head

It fell into a basket like ripe fruit,
blood sluicing the chopping block,
eyes rolling, lips a parting kiss.

When women fear one another,
deep mistrust is a kind of fuel,
feeding ferocious fires that burn

without boundaries, untamed.
Mary's blood couldn't stain her
or rouge her cheeks in death.

The axe fell twice and she lost
the auburn trophy of deceit,
her crowning glory come adrift.

Mary's tresses, just another lie;
to lose your head, windfall fruit
falling, just another way to die.

*Mary Queen of Scots 1542 – 1587 reigned over Scotland until her
forced abdication. Her life was complicated by politics and
religion and she was eventually executed, although even this
took two blows of the axe. When her executioner lifted up her
head to show the crowd, the queen suffered further ignominy as
her auburn wig fell off revealing her own short grey hair.*

Mary Whitehouse returns with a view to doing some *research*

Naturally she takes the back stairs, under cover
of darkness, wearing shades and a hat. The plan
is to bear witness to current morality, hang out,
get a feel for depravity and take it from there.

To say she is shocked is to imagine what the Pope
might think about his priests selling spice or nuns
signing up to Tinder. She gets home tired from
watching people flirt from pub to pub to club.

Mary turns on the telly, flicks through channels,
is confronted with flesh and fucking; swearing
seems a lexicon of unimaginable words burning
into her white skin like gaudy inflamed tattoos.

Following advice from the worldly-wise, Mary
knows what's needed. Reaching into the pocket
of her jeans, she finds the baccy and rolls a joint.
Clouds return her to a peaceful place; it's Heaven.

*Mary Whitehouse 1919 – 2001 campaigned against social
liberalism and the permissive society. She often criticised the
BBC and newspapers for what she believed were attacks on
morality and Christian values.*

Angel

Who knew she was so small in silver,
for placing at the top of the tree.
Who knew her wings might break,
mons pubis exposed in a park.

Who knew such a blessed Mary
would be served in such a way.
Who knew how immaculate
a statue was surely meant to be.

Who knew such a shining image
could be dulled with controversy.
Who knew these female forms
melting down into the ground.

Who knew she was so small in silver,
sculptured present from the past.
Who knew the unveiling of an angel
for placing at the top of the tree.

*Mary Wollstonecraft 1759 – 1797, writer, philosopher and
advocate of women's rights, died eleven days after giving birth
to her second daughter, Mary Shelley, author of 'Frankenstein'.
A controversial silver-coloured statue of Mary Wollstonecraft
was unveiled in 2020. It depicts a strangely small, totally naked
figure, melting into rather nebulous shapes at the base.*

Children, my children

Some mothers are inventors without wombs;
they brew their offspring in test tubes, freeze
eggs, add favourite blood to disguise mistakes.

And what a mistake! See how my boy rises up,
thinks himself a resurrection come to my rescue.
I might dare to love him, complex as Jocasta.

Our children march out into the world, electric,
charged with changing things. They are wired,
fragrant with our dreams, ready to ruin everything.

Mary Shelley 1797 – 1851, daughter of Mary Wollstonecraft, wrote the gothic novel 'Frankenstein'. The story is about a scientist who invents a creature made of body parts from cadavers, and brought to life by electricity. The monster craves human companionship and resents his creator with disastrous consequences. Mary is buried in a churchyard in Bournemouth, where I used to play as a child, my father pointing out her grave to me one day between games of football.

The lady down the food bank seems quite nice

She is the first face you see, the woman down the food bank.
She hands you two plastic bags straining at the handles.
She doesn't say much, maybe *hello* or *there you go.*

I think about her as I unpack the first bag, all tins and packets.
I noticed her eyes today; they weren't avoiding me as such but
I know she couldn't bring herself to look at me for long.

She is kind I suppose, to turn up every week and do this stuff.
She is behind the line of tables, apart from us, set back.
She gives us our share, our allotted pasta, beans, soups.

I only ever mouth a thin *thank you* like it's been prised out of me.
I wonder if she smokes or drinks, if she has a husband or a cat.
I have more and more questions every time I see her.

She is turning into an avatar in my game of *what's for dinner.*
She has grown wings and moves on monstrous metal legs.
She makes a noise like a giant tin-opener, wrenches away lids.

I will offer her my children as collateral for the occasional smile.
I will tell her what she craves, that she is *nice,* that I love her.
I will swap places with her for a day, just one short 24 hour day.

She accidentally touches my skin and her hands mutate into weapons.
She has claws that snag the carriers, spilling donated food like rocks.
She screams clanging bells of abuse, twists on her hinged heels.

I am falling backwards, tins bruising me as they hail and clatter.
I am drowning in own brands, labels peeling off, silencing my cries.
I love you nice lady, you are good, I will remember you always.

She is the last face you see, the woman down the food bank.
She asks you to sign for the two bags before you leave.
She notices your arms are scratched. You pull down your sleeves.

Lady Mary Cornelia Vayne-Tempest (1828-1906) much-beloved by her community for her charitable work including regular distribution of food and clothing to the poor near her home in Machynlleth, Powys. The townsfolk paid to have a commemorative bust of her made after her death. It is rare for a woman in Wales to have such a sculpture commissioned through voluntary subscriptions and is a real demonstration of the high regard her community had for her.

As a nation, we have always been divided by class, wealth and privilege, maybe now more than ever. However, Lady Mary seems to have had genuine concern for those of little means and the people loved her for it in return. Her obituary in The Cambrian News read "her tact was great and she was alike in word and silence."

the medicine goes down

i want to fly with you and have you be my **mother**
we could feed the birds **you and i** tell one another
stories i like stories and dancing and falling **asleep**
in your lap and hearing you sing lullabies of love
i want you to look after me like a real live mother
the one who didn't die the one who keeps me **safe**
from angry fathers from fathers who meant well
from fathers who can't let go please be my mother
just a spoonful of you and **the medicine** goes down
you are **so sweet** so sickly sweet you are not real
but i love you only you can make her come back
i need her more than i ever have please help me
to get her back i need her back soon **before i die**
before it's too late sickly sweet surrogate mother

*Mary Poppins was a book series written by P L Travers which
was made into the 1964 musical film produced by Walt Disney.
The film is set in Edwardian London and follows the fantasy of a
nanny, Mary Poppins, who has super powers. She helps a rich,
somewhat absent father who works in a bank, to see that money
is not everything. The film came out around the time I lost my
own mother when I was just five, so the character had deep
appeal to me as a child.*

Tredegar time

Here time was once measured entirely in iron,
ticking along powered by bars and rods and rails.
Seconds were smelted, hours blasted, days
soon abandoned, converted into heritage sites
for tourists and school trips. But the brass band,
some male voices, keep their own time, pulse beats
in halls to baton tempo. And there's a clock of iron,
Mary's clock, that stands the test of Tredegar time.
She looks on from her bench, the street air circulating
where once she choked for breath, tuberculosis death
taking her so very young, early, ahead of her time.
Tredegar time is taller than most, stretches to skies,
pulls the gaze upward, chimes with high expectation.
Tredegar time is built on a woman's vision, imagination.

*Mary Elizabeth Davis 1825 – 1857, wife of Richard who managed
the Tredegar ironworks. Mary died of a lung haemorrhage before
the fundraising bazaar for the clock tower planned by her and her
sister could take place. There is a commemorative metal bench for
Mary facing the clock, considered the tallest of its kind, which she
was so keen to see erected, so Mary lives on in these Tredegar
landmarks.*

Mr Eliot

It was *Mr* Eliot as far as I was concerned,
why would I have reason to think otherwise.
Mrs Stockwell had us reading a page each,
voices trailing round the classroom until
my turn, my pleasure to read at long last.

I couldn't understand why some dreaded
the call to read, shuddered inside as voices
got nearer. At least we *could* read, not like
some of them in his books; poor urchins
ground into the land like country fossils.

When I found out George was a woman
I felt betrayed. She had hidden amongst
the rows of desks, cowering like a nervous
reader, afraid of her higher pitch, cheating
us into thinking a man had such imagination.

This was a girls' grammar school, ambition
shone out of us like a hundred bright moons.
We were destined for doctor's brass plaques,
business cards, trophies, even book shelves.
Your turn George, Georgie, Georgina Eliot.

*Mary Ann Evans 1819 – 1880 used the pseudonym George Eliot to
write her novels because she wanted to be taken seriously as a
writer, and wanted to prevent public scrutiny of her private life,
including her relationship with a married man. As a teenage
school student studying her literature, I was horrified to learn
George Eliot was actually a woman, and could not understand the
deceit.*

Five disciplines

They run amok along the Springfield Road
throwing petrol bombs and stones at police;
you ran a mile and sprinted to Olympic gold,
not a stone's throw, but *citius, altius, fortius*.

They set vehicles alight, offer sectarian abuse,
kids who know nothing of the passed troubles;
you a trustee of Outward Bound know the value
of letting off steam up in Antrim's Black Mountain.

They jump to the beat of men who would stir it,
get used and abused in their cycle of old hatred;
you are honoured for your service, your triumph
against the odds over five golden disciplines.

*Mary Peters was born in 1939 and famously competed for GB &
NI winning a gold medal for Pentathlon in the 1972 Munich
Olympics. She represented NI at the Commonwealth Games
many times, winning gold at Pentathlon and Shot Put, and was
a real inspiration to me as a child. I went on to train as a P.E.
Teacher and remember Mary taking the warm-ups when I used
to run in the Liverpool 10k road races. Mary became Vice
President of the NI Outward Bound Association and championed
young able-bodied and disabled NI athletes through the Mary
Peters Trust. At the time of writing, there had been a disturbing
resurgence of sectarian rioting in and around Belfast, with much
of the trouble perpetrated by very young people recruited by
older agitators.*

The voodoo of loss

They burn your rights over a flame,
turn civil liberties to ash. Ashen
you rise. Risen you fight for others.
Others need to learn. Learning
is denied. Denial is a voodoo.

The voodoo of loss is a bad spell,
burning your fingers, turning
fortunes to ash. Ashen you die.
Dying you are forgotten. Forgetting
is too easy. Easy is a voodoo.

I write a poem about you black Mary,
try to ignite your flame again.
Gaining remembrance is a truth.
Truth never lies. Lying is ash.
Ashen memory is the voodoo of loss.

*Mary Ellen Pleasant c1810-1904 a Black American who married
into money and made wise investments after her husband's
early death. She became a powerful woman championing civil
rights, especially those of African Americans treated unfairly by
the justice system. However, her luck changed when she
supported a case that ended up hurting her both financially and
politically. Mary's situation really fell apart with the death of
her financial partner and the ensuing dispute with his widow.
Ultimately she lost her vast fortune and died in poverty,
tarnished by accusations in the press of everything from murder
to casting voodoo spells.*

Lady Mary inoculates her young son in 1718

No death for you my tiny boy, not this way.
Today I deliberately infect you with the pox,
safe in the knowledge that this madness works.

And yet, and yet, to see you cut this way,
to see such badness introduced, is to face
my own death a million times or more.

No death for you my tiny boy, not this way.
I watch and wait, share the small fever,
the smaller blisters as they rise then fade.

And yet, and yet, the scars are on my face,
the price of survival, to be marked this way.
Husband, see how our son sings and plays.

No death for you my tiny boy, not this good day.
The Turkish custom I have witnessed
I will pack in my Ottoman trunk, bring home.

And yet, and yet, who will trust me and believe,
take their own poison to avoid such plague,
how men will come to see this strange wisdom.

No death for you around the world in coming days;
syringes full of vaccine to keep sicknesses at bay.
We watch and wait as new science plays it's part.

And yet, and yet, the politics and prejudice
still needles and infects. But no death or scars
for you my tiny boy; soon you will grow immune.

Lady Mary Wortley Montagu 1689 – 1762, an English aristocrat who lost her brother to smallpox. Lady Mary also contracted the disease but recovered just before moving to what was Constantinople, now Istanbul, to accompany her husband who had been made Ambassador to the Ottoman Empire. Here Lady Mary encountered Turkish women and their practice of using pus infected with smallpox to effectively inoculate against the disease. Back home in England, Lady Mary even allowed her physician to use this treatment to inoculate first her son and later her daughter. Lady Mary's bravery and pioneering actions were the pre-cursor for Edward Jenner's work on vaccinations, not that Lady Mary received much credit for this at the time.

Nurse in the shadows

The pathology of sickness is an epidemic of shadows
on skin, on tissue, on lungs, on wards. Cures flicker,
colour blind, lights immune to where you come from.

In her Sevastopol hotel, she nursed the dying soldiers,
brought comfort as battles raged; grasped the hands
of injured men as colour drained and blood ran out.

What darkness then to refuse her, to turn her down.
The pathology of prejudice is an epidemic of shadows
on skin, in hearts, in history if we turn a blind eye.

And what of nurses in the shadows of our wards,
their colour overlooked like Mary, racism a sickness
we need to cure with the light of a million lamps.

*Mary Seacole 1805-1881 overcame prejudice to play an
important role supporting soldiers during the Crimean War.
Despite her huge knowledge and experience of cholera and other
epidemics, her application to go to the Crimea to deploy her
nursing skills was turned down by the War Office. Her mixed
race heritage was clearly a factor and she was forced to use
private resources to set up a hotel near Sevastopol, from which
she attended to the sick and wounded. The end of the war left her
financially bankrupt but veterans raised thousands of pounds to
help her. However, her reputation soon faded after her death
and it is only in more recent times that her achievements have
once again been acknowledged, indeed championed and
celebrated.*

The Ballad of Stagecoach Mary

Dressed like a man and carrying two guns,
Mary needed no one to tell her how to be.
Stagecoach Mary, quick-shooting bodyguard,
once a slave, now free, with new identity.

Dressed like a man and carrying two guns,
Mary dark of skin stood out on the trail.
Stagecoach Mary, like a big old grizzly bear,
kept thieves away when carrying the mail.

Mary dark of skin stood out on the trail,
hard drinking carrier on the Star Route.
Mary of the Wild West, guns always ready,
you'd have to take her on to get the loot.

Hard drinking carrier on the Star Route,
Stagecoach Mary could outshoot the best.
She kept mail and money safe from harm,
her gun-slinging put all outlaws to the test.

Dressed like a man and carrying two guns,
once a slave, now free, with new identity.
Stagecoach Mary had the Wild West beat,
no one to tell her how she ought to be.

*Mary Fields, born a slave around 1832, was an African
American woman who worked in a convent after she was
released from slavery. However, her masculine appearance and
behaviour, which included heavy drinking, smoking and
shooting guns, got her kicked out of the convent. She turned her
gun handling skills to good use by getting a job as a mail carrier
in the Wild West, where she gained a fierce reputation. The
ballad form, which always tells a story and which uses a strict
rhyme pattern and repetition, seems fitting in order to celebrate
this legendary character.*

Quite contrary

This was the only place she felt at peace,
our Mary, in her haphazard back garden.
She loved to tend it, plant things to grow,
fashioned a path like a rosary from stones.
She rubbed slate together trying for sparks
but found instead she could draw patterns.
Mary avoided cracks and spaces between,
afraid she might disappear. She lingered
on the flat rounds, safe holy wafer discs,
dissolved old troubles on her salty tongue.
At the end of the garden, a rotting wooden
shed for self-harm and tears on bad days.
She never could understand how the hell
she was supposed to hear the sea in shells.

*Mary, Mary, Quite Contrary was an English nursery rhyme
circa 1744. The words are often thought to have religious and
historical significance and the Mary they refer to may be any of
Mary Mother of God, Mary Queen of Scots or even Mary Tudor.*

She sells seashells

She plucked twists of ammonites from the shore
yet men could not get their tongues around
Mary being female. She spun her skirts about
those fossilised men of science, saved the truth
from stormy seas after landslides. Mary dug deep
for bones that offered up the secrets of the past.

Today another Mary digs in Dorset sand and shale,
inhales the salty air, looks up the cliff face to the sky
where cloud patterns swirl and dance. She can dream
a PhD in Palaeontology, piece together all her finds.
She discovers your footsteps, has mastered the words,
she sells seashells on the seashore, and her tongue
twists no more to closed door cabinets of curiosity.
Mary is discovered, found, made whole, unfurled.

*Mary Anning, pioneering palaeontologist and fossil collector
1799-1847, who was shunned by the Geological Society of
London for being female and a Dissenter, a Protestant Christian.
It has been suggested that the tongue-twister 'she sells seashells
on the seashore' was written about Mary Anning, as she did
indeed sell some of the fossils she found.*

Dreamgirl

My dreams are diva dreams in sequins and high heels,
big hair and hair bands, touring, touring. My dreams
come in threes, one more stand-out than the others.
My dreams start in black and white, burst into color
on billboards and TV specials. My dreams sing
backing vocals, sway to a Motown beat, alto tone
longing to lead. My dreams are rivalry and tension,
Come See About Me, the trouble with threesomes.
My dreams are Detroit diva dreams in the motor city,
glamorous amongst the grease monkeys, girlie dreams,
that glitter you awake. My dreams are gowns and wigs,
dressing room doors with stars, touring, touring dreams
that wear you down and leave you out. My dreams
are choreographed and crowded, dreams of stardom,
top spot dreams in lights and headlines. My dreams
are sleek and sexy, long lashes fluttering dreams,
dresses slit and ebony thighs exposed. My dreams
are dancing diva dreams, lost harmony, wrong note
dreams with added rumour dreams. My dreams sing
with or without you, are reach number one dreams,
break records dreams, fall out of favour dreams.
My dreams are diva dreams in sequins and high heels,
big hair and hair bands, touring, touring. My dreams
are supreme dreams, *Come See About Me* dreams,
Some Day We'll be Together dreams, those dreams.

*Mary Wilson 1944 – 2021 was a founding member of the
American, record-breaking,1960s, girl group The Supremes.
Mary often felt overlooked by her rival Diana Ross who left the
trio to pursue her career as a solo artist and actress. Mary did
have her own long and successful career which included
keeping The Supremes going with various singers in the line-
up. She also wrote a number of best-selling books, including
her autobiography 'Dreamgirl'.*

If I knew you were coming

Take a bowl and clouds of flour,
sweetness, fat, eggs to bind;
more than anything, add air.

The oven is ready and I watch
you slowly rise, magic chemistry
at work, performing miracles.

You are brown and glistening
like babies baked in batches
twelve at a time, smelling golden.

If I knew you were coming
maybe the baking would
have been laid aside.

I might have prepared differently;
not this flowery apron, bare hands,
this list of instructions

but better PPE, and oxygen,
much more air to make you rise.

*Mary Berry, born 1935, was at the time of writing well into her
80s, and is one of the so-called celebrity cooks and bakers who
frequent our television screens. During the lockdown, necessary
because of the Covid crisis, many people took to learning new
skills such as baking. Whilst this is of course no bad thing, it is
perhaps interesting to note the stark contrast in priorities with
those of NHS workers, many of whom found themselves with
inadequate personal protective equipment and dwindling
oxygen supplies.*

Rainbow

After Mary Ruefle's 'color pieces' about which she says, "if you substitute the word happiness for the word sadness, nothing changes"

Rainbow sadness is the sadness of low paid workers left to find their own pots of gold, on early morning and late night public transport, or on long walks home in all weathers. It is the sadness of not admitting you were at a pride march, opting instead to tell everyone you had a training course, had to babysit your sister's two year old or were booked onto some sort of spiritual retreat. Rainbow sadness forms a perfect arch of all the other sadnesses, paints a Pink Floyd classic album cover, refracts the light like a boss and proves the importance of both sun and rain together in the big old sky. Rainbow sadness is not having to choose, is having it all, is basic primary school science made into pictures to stick on the fridge or keep to show the grandchildren a zillion years later. Rainbow sadness is light and bright, hopeful sadness, the kind of sadness you can bear once you get used to it, have hatched a plan, learned some coping skills and embraced the adjustment needed. Rainbow sadness is frankly too much, whilst never being enough and causing no end of confusion, so much so you try to stuff it in a box but it keeps escaping like blood from a deep cut or water in your cupped hands. Rainbow sadness hurts your eyes, flirts with oil and bird feathers and makes too many damn promises to be believable, especially when it mimics itself, doubling up right in front of you, almost within touching distance of every artist ever to stand at an easel facing an empty white canvas.

Mary Ruefle, born 1952, is an American poet and finalist in the 2020 Pulitzer Prize. She has published over a dozen books of poetry and has won many awards. Mary Ruefle is a poet I have come to admire greatly for her dark and witty writing, her close observation of the world, and her ability to capture all life's strangeness in extraordinarily relatable simplicity.

The family of things

Your family is carefully, chaotically arranged like a virtual orchestra,
playing tunes and great overtures to the beat of every creatures's heart.
The world calls you to listen and be moved, to let yourself tune in,
flap your wings in chorus with wild geese looming overhead.

We watch their flight, marvel at their synchronicity, are drawn into
the rapture of their swelling number, high over the cool lake below.
Moving as one, they carry us, a surge of feathers quivering like bows
drawn over strings, their stretched necks the frets of instruments.

The family of things is an arrangement in many parts, each paced
and composed to cancel the discordant, clashing babble of machines;
a place where you and I fit in organically like the cries of geese,
first loud, raucous, then a decrescendo slow and deliberate and free.

*Mary Oliver 1935 – 2019, an American poet who took much of
her inspiration from the natural world. She was greatly
influenced by Edna St Vincent Millay. In 1983 she won the
Pulitzer Prize and she continued as a prolific, visionary and
much-quoted writer well into old age. In her poem, Wild Geese,
she said, "whoever you are...the world...calls to you like the wild
geese...over and over announcing your place in the family of
things".*

Being kind

I am the white kind   the brown kind   the black kind

you are kindred to me   I am the female kind   the male kind

the other kind   you are kindred to me   I am the whole kind

the b r o k e n kind   you are kindred to me   I am any kind

you are kindred to me   I am the kind kind   I am the nasty kind

you are kindred to me   I am the beyond reach kind   do you know this kind

you are still kindred to me   I am the learning kind   I am the vacant kind

you are kindred to me   I am trying to be kind   does this change your mind

you are kindred to me   kindred kind   kind kindred   follow me follow me

be kind to me   be kindred to me   I am the coming with you kind   always

Mary Sawyer c1800
The story goes that Mary from Massachusetts was looking after a lamb
rejected by its mother. Not wanting to be parted from her pet lamb, Mary took
it to school where it received a mixed welcome. The poem we now know as the
children's nursery rhyme 'Mary had a little lamb' was designed to teach the
morality of kindness, especially towards animals.

Acknowledgements

The two Marys meet for a catch-up and *Quite contrary* were first published in *Kissing in the Dark* by Pat Edwards (Indigo Dreams, 2020).

Mr Eliot was first published in *An Insubstantial Universe - A poetry anthology in celebration of George Eliot* on the bicentenary of her birth' - Edited by Edwin Stockdale and Amina Alyal (Yaffle, 2020).